Published in Great Britain in MMXXI by
Scribblers, an imprint of
The Salariya Book Company Ltd
25 Marlborough Place, Brighton BN1 1UB
www.salariya.com

ISBN: 978-1-913971-03-8

© The Salariya Book Company Ltd MMXXI

All rights reserved. No part of this publication may be reproduced, stored in or introduced into a retrieval system or transmitted in any form, or by any means (electronic, mechanical, photocopying, recording or otherwise) without the written permission of the publisher. Any person who does any unauthorised act in relation to this publication may be liable to criminal prosecution and civil claims for damages.

1 3 5 7 9 8 6 4 2

A CIP catalogue record for this book is available from the British Library.

This book is sold subject to the conditions that it shall not, by way of trade or otherwise, be lent, resold, hired out, or otherwise circulated without the publisher's prior consent in any form or binding or cover other than that in which it is published and without similar condition being imposed on the subsequent purchaser.

Editor: Nick Pierce

Visit
www.salariya.com
for our online catalogue and
free fun stuff.

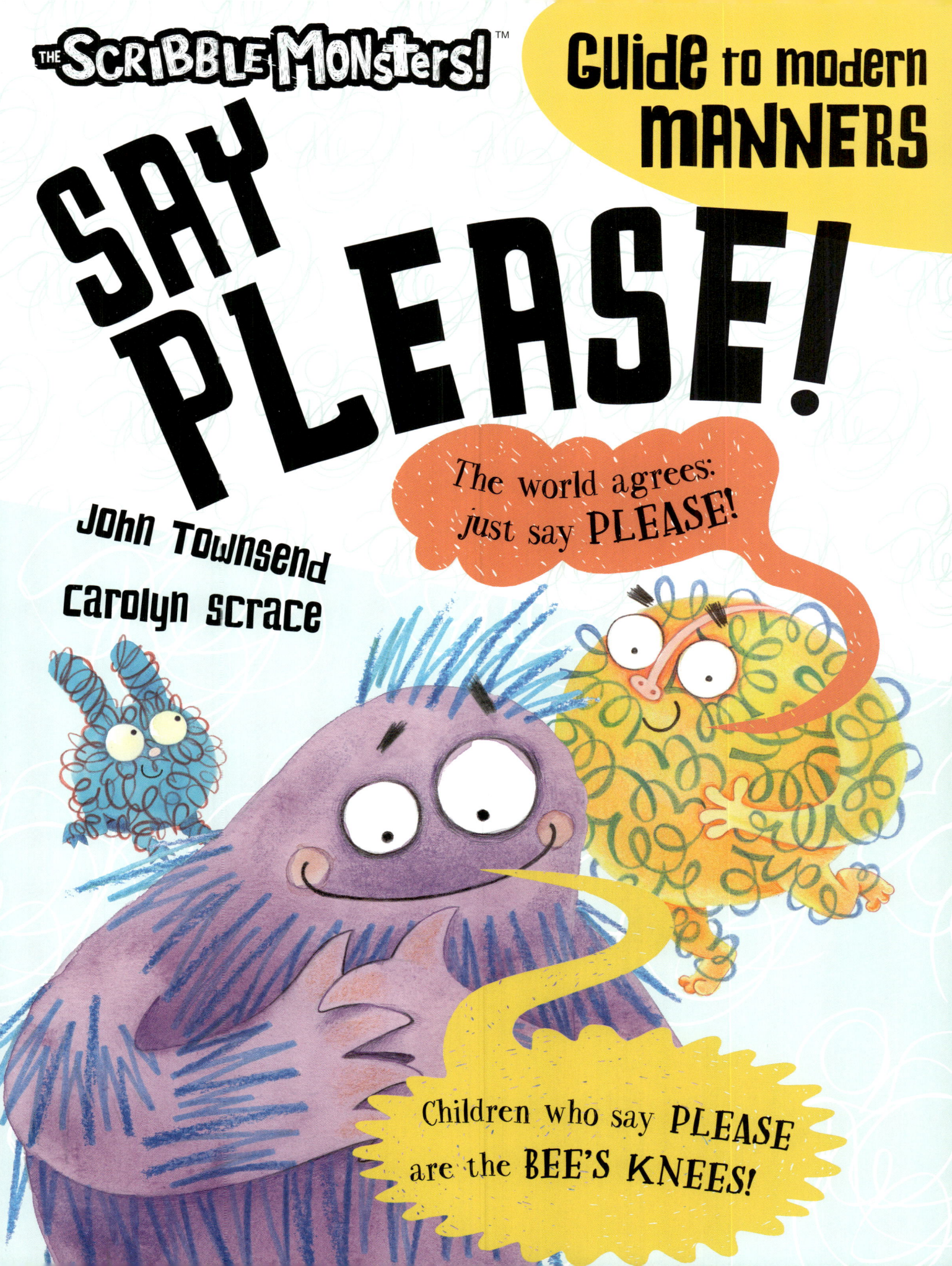

We're the friendly Scribble Monsters,
We scribble lots of lines
And write how manners can be fun
On all our scribbly signs.

Manners? Yes, please!

Please say please

What everyone agrees is:
we'll all say our pleases!

Some little children can forget
To leave kind words behind them...
We're here to scribble our advice
And find ways to remind them.

Smudge will always say a **'please'**,
When asking for some dinner.

I might not get it if I don't,
So **'please'** can be a winner!

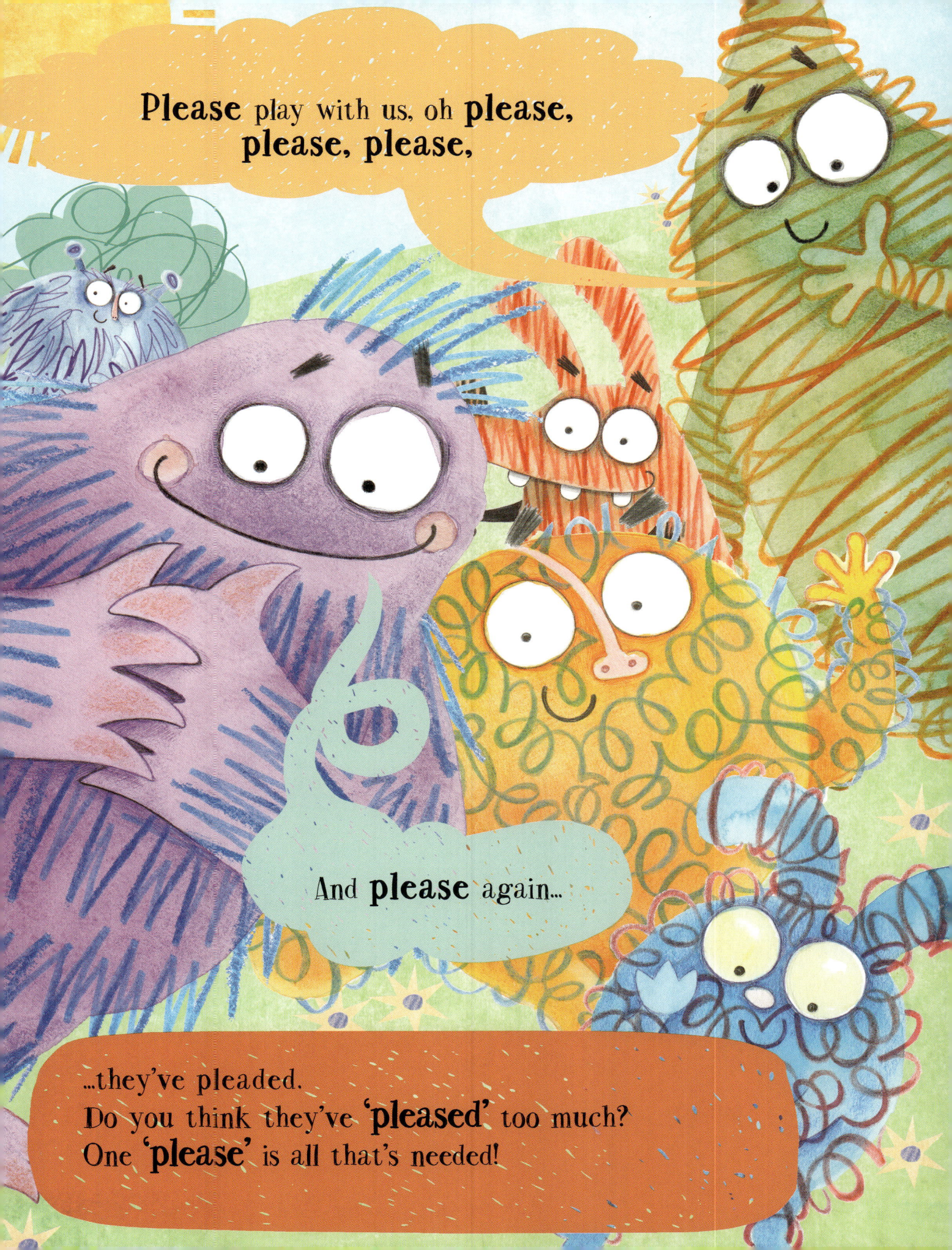

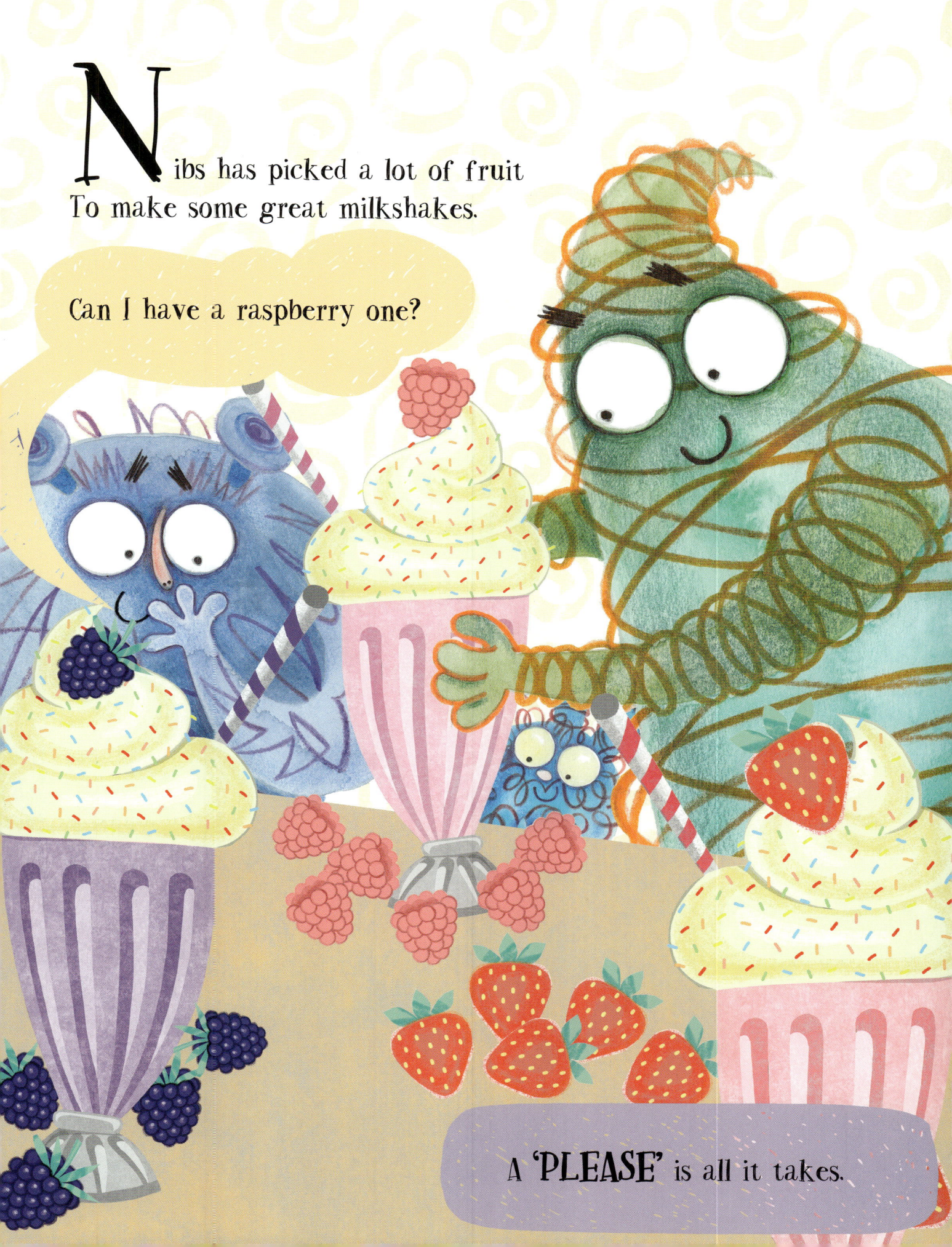

Nibs has picked a lot of fruit
To make some great milkshakes.

Can I have a raspberry one?

A 'PLEASE' is all it takes.

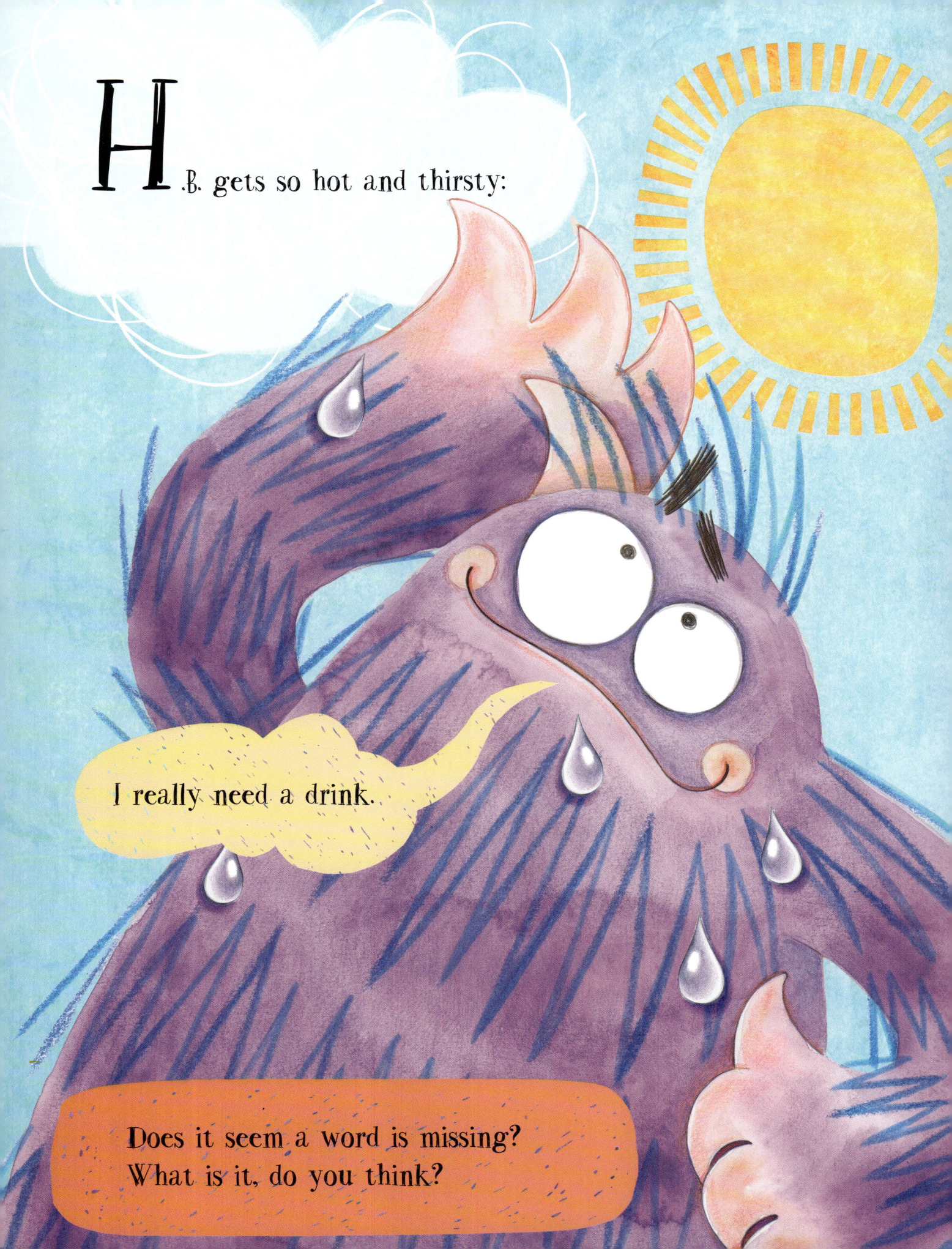

Nibs has trouble tying laces:

H.B., will you assist?

Has Nibs asked H.B. properly?
What word has Nibs just missed?

'PLEASE' is the word that does the trick,
'PLEASE' is the word to say
To show how we can be polite
And ask the proper way.

Children who remember manners
And don't forget their 'PLEASES'
Make the Scribble Monsters dance
And hug with cuddly squeezes!

H.B., Inky, Nibs and Pablo,
Blot and Smudge – all these
Want to be your friends forever
And shout a big, loud **'PLEASE!'**

CAN YOU HELP US FIND THE ANSWERS TO THIS QUIZ?

QUESTION 1

We give awards to children who do what?

QUESTION 2

When I said 'Please can I go out to play for half an hour precisely?' did Pablo let me?

QUESTION 3

I asked Blot if he wanted a toasted sandwich. Blot said 'Yes, I would'. What else should he have said?

QUESTION 4

When I am thirsty, should I say 'I really need a drink NOW!'...?

Look at the last page of the book to see if you are right!

MORE MONSTER QUESTIONS

QUESTION 5

When I ask H.B. to help me tie my laces, what word have I forgotten to say?

QUESTION 6

When I want some peas, should I just say 'Pass them over here'?

QUESTION 7

What makes us all dance and hug with cuddly squeezes?

THE WORLD AGREES – JUST SAY CHEESE!

QUESTION 8

Which word is wrong on my flag?

Look at the last page of the book to see if you are right!